Yesterday
Today
and
Tomorrow
Too

Written By: Cheyanne Cramm

ISBN: 978-1-7389116-0-8

Printed in the United States of America

Preface

No one's life is like anyone else's. We all go through things, be it good or bad. This book is a collection of my poems and thoughts. My goal is to help and inspire people, including you. I want you to know that no matter what life might throw at you, you've got this. I hope that you find what you need, or who you might need, to help you in your moment.

Life isn't meant to be easy.
Life experiences is what build character.
What you decide is up to you.

I am putting spaces in this book in hopes, to one day, make this world just a little bit better and to help those who need just a little help and encouragement. Know that you are not alone out there no matter what you are going through in life. Anything is possible, you are worth every effort you put forth.

I was encouraged by my oldest son to write a book. I started in 2019. Life happened, and I acknowledged that that was okay. But I got back on track and worked hard. Here's to every year moving forward. I hope you all live your life to how you want.

Much love,

Cheyanne

Table of contents

From Shadows to light

When I look at you,
The shadow fades away, and the light sparkles in your eyes.

You blink,
Those lashes flutter,
That grin turns into a smile.
Ask yourself, where have you been for so long?
You were always there, but just in the shadows.

Now you've stepped back into the light.
Now it's your time to shine.
Now you've been seen and found.
There will no longer be a shadow in front of you,
Always behind.

Make every step forward better than the last.
Take but, a moment.
Close your eyes and embrace the warm light that life is about to bring into your life.

This is you,
You're that person.
The person who has stepped out of the shadow and back into the light.
Embrace you,
Love you.
Live like no one is watching.

This space is for you to reflect on a time when you felt like you were in a dark place.

_____

_____

_____

_____

_____

_____

_____

_____

_____

_____

_____

_____

_____

_____

_____

_____

_____

Hands

Interlock your hands with mine,

They fit perfectly together.

A reminder that I am right by your side.

Whether we meet halfway

Or

I meet you and you meet me.

Trust that when we connect, I will not let you go.

I will always keep you in front of me so that you know I am, and always will be behind

you every step of the way.

Take your time,

And do not rush,

Our hands are interlocked.

We are right where we need to be.

Soft but firm grip of my hand will remind you that,

I will always keep you safe.

When the road looks rough or

The path is narrow.

Interlock your hand with mine.

With one step at a time,

I will be behind you

Every

S

T

E

P

Of the way.

Challenge

Hands is about holding someone's hand and helping them know that you're there for them.

The next time someone in your life is feeling down. Hold their hand. How do they respond?

Did it help? Did they feel any better?

_____

_____

_____

_____

_____

_____

_____

_____

_____

_____

_____

_____

_____

_____

_____

That look

For all the fears you have inside your head,
Look into my eyes.

Know that when I look at you,
I am looking at the whole you,
I want those fears to realize that it will be okay.
Those fears to realize,
That I will not run away.

When all those worries and doubts
Come into your mind,
Remember how I looked at you.
Know that when I look at you, I see you.
The whole you.
Day by day, and with one foot in front of the other
I hope those fears will become but a distant memory.

But when you look into my eyes,
I want you to see me.
For I too, have the same fears.

Self-reflection

Have you had someone look at you and make you feel just a little bit better? Do you know of a time where you did that for someone else?

_____

_____

_____

_____

_____

_____

_____

_____

_____

_____

_____

_____

_____

_____

_____

_____

_____

Changes

Changes can happen,
You can let them.

You can control if they are positive or negative.

You decide what you want in your life,
Those changes are yours to make.

We need to take life day by day,
Embrace what life we want for ourselves.

Make the choices,
make the changes,
and,
take one step at a time.

They will not happen overnight.
Remind yourself to be patient.

Changes take time,
but they can happen.
Changes will happen,
If you accept to let them.

We all want to make changes in our lives. What are some that you are working towards, and list them in importance to you.

_____

_____

_____

_____

_____

_____

_____

_____

_____

_____

_____

_____

_____

_____

_____

_____

_____

_____

Time

When you receive someone's time,
Accept it gracefully.

Appreciate it.
Hold onto it.

Give time in return.
Give it wholeheartedly.

Because for every minute we don't,
That's a minute we have lost.

The minutes lost cannot be regained nor found.

Make every breath count,
Smile every smile fully.

Enjoy every moment you get.

If you're not provided the time,
Don't settle.

Time can be taken away at any moment.
Appreciate it.

Hold onto it.

Take some extra time for people in your life.

List some people in your life that you haven't seen in a while. Let's be honest; we all live our own lives. Name some people and make just a little time for each one. Just one person extra in each month. Not too much to ask for.

_____

_____

_____

_____

_____

_____

_____

_____

_____

_____

_____

_____

_____

_____

_____

_____

_____

Take a look

Take a look.

Do you see what I see?

Listen.

Do you hear what I hear?

Talk.

Do you know what my words are?

Breathe.

Can you feel me breathe?

If you see, don't let go.

Hold on tight.

If this is what you want,

GO FOR IT!

This is your life to live!

Make the most of it!

Work hard for the things you want.

But first,

Look in the mirror.

And look.

Self love

This is a self-love section for you. Let's bring it to the table.

Acknowledge some fears you have.

Acknowledge some dreams you have.

Acknowledge things about yourself you don't love.

Acknowledge some things about yourself that you love.

_____

_____

_____

_____

_____

_____

_____

_____

_____

_____

_____

_____

_____

_____

Everywhere

I am here.

Right here looking at you.

Watching you grow and achieve great things.

Not knowing where the future.

Will take me or you,

But I will be there.

Right there,

Looking at you.

But for now,

Take my hand;

Let's walk a while.

Down this path called life.

I know there will be hills.

On this path,

But you will climb them.

Step

     By

          step.

I am here.

Right here.

        Always was and always will be.

This page will be open for what ever you want it to be for.

Free

They will keep you warm,

They will keep you safe.

They will hold you up,

When you feel like falling.

Wings

Spread your wings into the wonderful world.

Spread your wings

And

Embrace what life has to offer you.

Wings

They will be your shelter.

They will be your greatest escape.

Your wings will take you to where

You need to go and be.

When a feather falls,

Let it set you free.

Show yourself what it means to feel free

Rain

When I stand here,

I think about what I was,

And what I will become.

Looking around me to take in what surrounds me.

As the sun shines,

The rain begins to fall.

Do I stay or do I go?

The decision is mine to make.

Hold out my arms,

Lift my chin,

And twirl.

Let the rain fall.

As each sweet droplet runs down my forehead,

I know to accept this as nothing less than a gift.

A gift that will help me grow.

I slow down and stop.

The sun begins to peak through the cloud.

Bright child, don't let the rain make you go.

The rain will only bring you what you need to grow.

Have you ever danced in the rain? Have you ever run in the rain? How did you feel

about what was going on in that moment? Try it! Make someone else do it with you!

Smile

When she walks into a room,
It's the first thing you'll notice.

Her smile.

Pure and full of life.
When she looks at you,
You will know that she's true.

It will beam from cheek to cheek.
And radiate from her eyes.

Purposely, she will give to anyone who needs her.
Selflessly.

Her smile.

Will always make a difference in someone's life.
If you are in her presence,
Make sure you notice it.
For if you don't,
that glow will fade.

Her smile.
Her Bright, Beautiful, Caring,
Smile.

Go out this week and make 20 people smile. Take note of 20 people that have made you smile.

_____

_____

_____

_____

_____

_____

_____

_____

_____

_____

_____

_____

_____

_____

_____

_____

_____

_____

_____

_____

Power

It's in you, just breathe.

Take a good look in the mirror and absorb it.

Feel it.

Powerful.

You are amazing.

You are incredible.

You are desirable.

You are unstoppable.

Build, grow, and perform

To your greatest potential.

Don't let the fear of the shadows.

behind you take it away.

Take a leap.

Put one foot in front of the other.

Ignite it

Don't settle for anything less.

Always remember,

You

Are the power in you.

Make a list of words that make you feel powerful.

Now take those words and either print them, or put them places as a daily reminder. Do things in your day that make you feel powerful.

_____

_____

_____

_____

_____

_____

_____

_____

_____

_____

_____

_____

_____

_____

_____

_____

_____

_____

Space

Where ever you are
Know that you are in control of that space.

My space is what I create,
and where I create it.
Who we let in and out of our space is also in our control.
When and if you are let into my space,
Don't take advantage of it.

When and if you let me into yours,
I will be nothing but what you need.

Space
Give it and take it.
If you want to give more of your space,
Say something.
If I want you to take more of my space,
I will say something.

But for now,
Keep the space the way it is.
Enjoy the space you are in.

We all need some space sometimes, and that's okay.

Make notes on some things that would make the spaces in your life more calm for you and make you content. Some examples might be; taking a relaxing bath, journalling, reading, going for a walk, yoga, etc.

_____

_____

_____

_____

_____

_____

_____

_____

_____

_____

_____

_____

_____

_____

_____

_____

_____

_____

Shadows

There's no light there.

Why must you stay?

Take your time, it is okay.

Do you know how beautiful you are?

This is not who you are.

This is not where you should be.

Just like a sunflower,

You should be out there,

With the sun shining on you.

Please don't back up.

Come with me and take my hand.

Take a chance and come out of the shadow.

You should not be hidden.

Flourish, grow, live, and be loved.

I'll reach for you,

Take my hand.

I'll spin you around.

Out of this shadow and into the light.

Where you deserve the spotlight.

We all have at least one time in our lives when we were not okay.

This space will be for any time that you're not okay. Just simply write down that you're not okay and a date. Take accountability and try and acknowledge how many days you were not okay and what went on in that day.

_____

_____

_____

_____

_____

_____

_____

_____

_____

_____

_____

_____

_____

_____

_____

_____

_____

_____

Can you see

Look at you,

Look how far you have come.

Look at where you are now.

Look at where you are going.

Stop.

Take in this moment.

You never take a break.

You are so focused.

Absorb all this love and energy, you are being given.

Look at her,

Look at where she's been.

Look at how far she's come.

Look at where she is now.

Look at where she is going.

Go

Go after her.

She won't stop.

She doesn't take breaks.

She is very focused.

Give her what she gives you,

And

Make her absorb it.

This is a progress check-in.

Show what you have accomplished for yourself this year. It might be as little as taking yourself out for lunch or getting a massage.

_____

_____

_____

_____

_____

_____

_____

_____

_____

_____

_____

_____

_____

_____

_____

_____

_____

_____

Best part of me

I will always be here.

Through the dark days

And the days the sun doesn't want to set.

I am patient.

Standing in a line is quite alright for me.

I won't get lost.

I'll take my time,

And get to where I need to be.

I don't rush life,

I will enjoy what I am given.

The best part of me,

Is all of me.

From my smile

To my laugh,

Even dancing in the kitchen.

The best part of me is often seen as I will always be here.

If you receive the opportunity,

To see the best of me,

You must bring it out in me.

Continue to be a part of the best of me.

What is your favorite characteristic about yourself, and why?

_____

_____

_____

_____

_____

_____

_____

_____

_____

_____

_____

_____

_____

_____

_____

_____

_____

_____

Because

If you knew all the answers,
If you'd seen all there was to see.

There would be nothing left.
Nothing to find out,
Nothing to learn.

No mistakes to be made,
You would not know.
Because that is not how life works.

You are not supposed to know the answers.
You are not supposed to see the unknown.
Learning every day is a gift.
Mistakes we make,
Show we are human.
Lessons in life show how we grow.
Every day we change in some way.
Just because.
All because that's how life works.

<u>Has there ever been a time in your life where you just simply said because?
Was there a time in your life where you just wanted to know the outcome
before even living the moment?</u>

_____

_____

_____

_____

_____

_____

_____

_____

_____

_____

_____

_____

_____

_____

_____

_____

Celebration

It's that time.
That time we have waited for.

For every minute we have waited,
All the steps we took to get here.

The two of us independently,
In our own zones,
Making each moment count.

And every minute better than the last.

The mountains I have climbed.
The mountains you have climbed,
For all the miles that were driven.

The tears that were shed,
The words exchanged,
All of the hard work put forth.

We did it!
We got to where we needed to be!
Hours of countless learning,
and growing.

It's that time.
The celebration.

Plan a celebration for your next milestone in your life. Some examples might be a birthday, graduation, promotion, just celebrate a success!

_____

_____

_____

_____

_____

_____

_____

_____

_____

_____

_____

_____

_____

_____

_____

_____

_____

_____

Bent

The angle

The direction

The feeling

How can a four-letter word be so complex?

A bend can be so smooth and yet thrilling.

Bent

Sounds sharp and in a space,

That's small and tight.

Is this what it's supposed to be like?

Even in the smallest,

Darkest of places

Being bent can be seen,

As a bend.

Go with what you feel,

And hang on.

Don't settle for being bent for too long.

Take a paperclip. Look at all the bends in it. But it still holds purpose.

Have one with you. Unbend it, rebend it. Make different shapes. Eventually, the metal will break, and that's okay. Those two pieces can still make two smaller paper clips. Note what you think of when doing this.

_____

_____

_____

_____

_____

_____

_____

_____

_____

_____

_____

_____

_____

_____

_____

_____

_____

_____

Believe

Beautiful one why does your chin hang low?
You have far too much in your soul to be this way.
Just believe.

Believe me when I say it will be alright,
That I will hold your hand,
And walk along with you.
Believe me when I say you are worth more,
Then I can give.
That I will give you everything,
Money cannot buy.

Believe ME when I say,
You are beautiful.
True beauty lies within our souls,
And yours simply radiates.

Believe me when I say,
You are stronger than you think.
Look over your shoulder for a moment,
and reflect on what you've overcome.

I believe in you and all that you are.
Now, you beautiful one
Must
Just believe.

What are some things that help you believe in yourself? How can you help someone else believe in themselves?

_____

_____

_____

_____

_____

_____

_____

_____

_____

_____

_____

_____

_____

_____

_____

_____

_____

_____

_____

_____

Chance

This is for you,
It's been there for a while now.

Would you like it?
Would you want it?
Will you try it?
Will it be enough for you?

Chance.

It will take you on incredible journeys,
But it can also make you learn some very valuable lessons.

Sometimes we don't get the choice of how life works,
But we do get the choice on the chances we are provided,
And what we decide to do.

Chance.

You will never know if you will get another.
Think wisely.
Think wholeheartedly.
Think consciously.
This is your chance to think.

Chance

Try something new. Take a chance. What are some things you have always wanted to try?

_____

_____

_____

_____

_____

_____

_____

_____

_____

_____

_____

_____

_____

_____

_____

_____

_____

_____

_____

She knows.

She sits there looking off into the distance.

She thinks.

I don't know how much more I can take.

Why must she go through this?

She is stronger than she looks.

She is stronger than she feels.

What she goes through makes her stronger.

It tests her patience,

It fires her anger,

It drives her motivation,

It fuels her soul.

She thinks.

Her thoughts are always changing,

Her mind is always going.

The many blessings in her life she is so thankful for.

She grows.

She blossoms.

She shines.

She sits there.

Knowing.

Knowing she can handle it.

How can you help someone you see is not in a good place?

Even if it's giving a homeless person a bottle of water, that bottle of water could show that person that they are worth living. Someone is out there and cares. Someone who they don't know.

_____

_____

_____

_____

_____

_____

_____

_____

_____

_____

_____

_____

_____

_____

_____

_____

_____

_____

Beside me

Wait for me.

I will not take long.

It is a process, but please be patient.

You want to hold my hand?

You want to walk with me?

You want to be by my side?

Just a minute,

I need to catch my breath,

This has never happened,

I don't know what to do.

I looked at you as you looked at me.

I smiled.

You waited for me.

You walked with me.

What more could a friend ask for?

Someone who chose to be there.

Who is your go-to when you need someone? Maybe that person is no longer alive. Remember, they can still help you get through your life. Show the world how they would want to see you living your life.

_____

_____

_____

_____

_____

_____

_____

_____

_____

_____

_____

_____

_____

_____

_____

_____

_____

_____

_____

_____

Wanted

That look in your eye,

The words from your lips,

And the way you hold me.

The feeling when we touch,

And the way we are when we're together.

Time provided,

And time taken.

That feeling of knowing you are wanted,

By the actions of others.

Words can express feelings.

"I want you here with me,

or I want to be there with you."

When actions are taken to make words a reality.

Wanted.

Is what you are.

Do you want this?

How does it feel?

Everyone wants to be wanted and accepted in this world. But we must start with wanting and accepting ourselves. Love ourselves. Go to a mirror and practice self-love.

Tell yourself you love you.

Tell yourself you are beautiful.

Tell yourself you know you have flaws.

Tell yourself you'll always try.

List some other self-love.

_____

_____

_____

_____

_____

_____

_____

_____

_____

_____

_____

_____

_____

_____

Enough

Will it ever be enough?
Will you ever be satisfied?
Take a long look in the mirror.
YES!

Yes, you will be enough.
Yes, you will be satisfied.

Every curve.
Every line.
Every wrinkle.
Every smile.
Every frown.

Every time you feel this way,
Take a long look in the mirror.

Say YES!

You are and will be all of these things.
Say it,
Say YES!
Know YES!
Feel YES!

You are enough,
You will be satisfied.

I miss you

Since the day you left,
My world has not been the same.

That smile.
Those dimples.
That heart that always gave.

I miss you.

I know the sun will still shine.
The wind will still blow,
And the seasons will continue to change.

But I miss you.

Every minute,
Of every day,
And every year.

I wish you could come back,
Just for me to see you one last time.
I miss you.
I will,
I will always miss you.

It's inevitable that someone in our lives will pass away. There will be at least one. There will be at least one day that will go by in which we will miss them. Talk about it. Talk about them. Their life might be gone, but their memory can still live. I'll leave extra space just in case.

_____

_____

_____

_____

_____

_____

_____

_____

_____

_____

_____

_____

_____

_____

_____

_____

_____

_____

_____

High

Distance,

Length,

Emotion.

Where do you hold yourself?

Reach,

Reach up.

High.

Go there.

Don't let anyone stop you.

Hold your head high.

No matter how long it takes to get there.

No matter what you go through,

Hold yourself high.

Climb every mountain,

Walk the path even if it seems long.

You will get there,

It might take some time.

But always,

Hold yourself high.

Hang on

Tight grip,

Loose grip.

It really doesn't matter.

As I sit here and you talk to me,

I hear your voice tremble.

All the worry and hurt in your voice.

Your breaths become quicker,

And your voice begins to race.

This mountain you are climbing is making you stronger.

Remember this.

Your words become quick sentences.

As the fear and other emotions start to flow out.

Hang on.

As I sit here in front of you,

I wrap my arm around you,

And hang on.

I will hang on until you need me to let go.

You can hang on until you need to let go.

Just having some space to journal and a place to leave your thoughts and emotions is not always a bad thing. Leave them here and get them off your chest.

_____

_____

_____

_____

_____

_____

_____

_____

_____

_____

_____

_____

_____

_____

_____

_____

_____

_____

Look up

Tiny lines in the pavement,

Sharp blades of grass,

Is the current view in your eyes?

Look up.

Look up and see what's in front of you,

Look up and see the positive in your life,

Look up and see the knowledge you've gained,

Look up and see how ambitious you are.

Look up.

You're missing out on so much right now,

Your thoughts are taking over,

Your getting lost and forgetting your potential.

Look up.

Look up at what this universe is trying to show you.

Look up because you deserve to see.

Look up because you need to see.

Look up so you can see.

Look up because life is about to make you,

Look up.

There is always a time or two in our lives when someone or something good happens. Here's a great place to share it!

_____

_____

_____

_____

_____

_____

_____

_____

_____

_____

_____

_____

_____

_____

_____

_____

_____

_____

Watch out

That path over there looks dark,
Are you sure you're okay?

I can't see you go there.
I won't watch you go there.

Watch out.

Can you see further that I can?
Should I go there?
If it's not safe, will you warn me?
Watch out.

Will you watch out for me as I will for you?

Watch out for the negative.
And guide me to the positive.

Watch out for the dark skies,
And shelter me from the rain.
Watch out for the wind,
And not let it take me away.
Watch out for the under toe,
And not let it take me under.

Watch out.

Watch out for me like I will you.

Who is someone in your life that you feel looks out for you?

Let them know that you are thankful. It might make them have a sense of being appreciated and wanted. Here's a space in case you don't know how to tell them.

_____

_____

_____

_____

_____

_____

_____

_____

_____

_____

_____

_____

_____

_____

_____

_____

You

Who are you?

Are you even sure?

Do you even know?

Take a minute.

Close your eyes.

Picture yourself at a young age.

With that bright, beautiful smile,

Running through a field.

Now open your eyes and look around.

Are you just as happy as you once were?

Are you the you that's the real you?

Are you happy with where you are?

Are you happy with who you are?

You are.

You are everything you want and more!

You are more than anyone deserves.

You are worth all the love and time you are provided.

You, yes, you!

So go, love you!

This is a place to see how you see yourself.

Try

I'll make breakfast.

I'll make lunch.

I'll make dinner.

I'll try for you.

I'll talk to you in the morning, afternoon, and night.

I'll include you in my everyday.

I'll drive for hours.

I'll try for you.

I will always try and show you I care.

I will try and make you see.

I will try and make you feel how I feel,

I'll try for you.

Even though this is all new to me.

When I look at you, I want to try.

I'll try for me,

But it's all for you.

Step by step, I know you'll do the same.

You already have.

All we do is try together.

She is

She is quiet.

She is fearful.

Sometimes, she feels numb by the pain of the past.

As she walks through that door,

She looks behind her.

She is no longer there.

She is no longer that girl.

She is bright,

She is loud, she is resilient,

She is bold,

She is beautiful.

She is more to this world than she thinks she is.

She has her doubts,

She has her worries.

But she is patient,

She is kind,

She is strong,

She is incredible.

She will be everything she wants to be and more.

She is who she is!

She is a self-reflection on who I am. Take this time and learn who you are.

_____

_____

_____

_____

_____

_____

_____

_____

_____

_____

_____

_____

_____

_____

_____

_____

_____

_____

_____

_____

Trust

The easiest thing to lose,

And the hardest thing to gain.

Should be made a priority every day.

Gained daily,

And not given away.

Each relationship grows with trust.

Lie and trust are gone.

Steal and trust are gone.

Don't communicate, and there will be a lack of trust.

When someone trusts you,

Know that they won't ask questions,

You will see it in their eyes,

Hear it in their voice,

And be shown by how they act.

Plant the seed of trust early on,

And watch it grow.

Work on that seed every day.

Hear my words,

See my actions,

Learn who I am.

I will show you how to trust again.

Having the life I have lived, it has had its ups and downs in the trust department. I try and give people the benefit of the doubt and trust sometimes more than I should. And to this day, it always comes at a price. Have you ever trusted someone and had that trust broken? Did you try and fix it or let them try? Or simply walk away?

_____

_____

_____

_____

_____

_____

_____

_____

_____

_____

_____

_____

_____

_____

_____

_____

I know

We don't get to know how our lives will go.

I know.

When life gets rough, it will be okay.

I know.

When I am calm and smile, life is good.

I know.

When I need help, you'll be there.

I know.

I know that with everything I am challenged in life,

I will get through.

I just know.

I have to just know.

Because.

Because if I don't know,

Then, I will crumble into a million different pieces.

Just like the leaves falling.

Day by day,

Each one until there is no more.

So today, and every day,

I remind myself.

I know.

I know because,

I can,

And I will.

Broken

Look over there.
See that piece,
See those down there,
All those pieces.

They should not be there.
Here's one,
And another.
All of them.

Pick them all up,
And put you back together.

They will all go back.
You will no longer be broken.

I am here.

Piece by piece,
You will be,
No longer,
Broken.

Feeling like we are falling apart is a part of life when what we are going through is tough. But a puzzle is never already put together when we buy them. They take time and each piece fits with many others. If glass is broken, those glass pieces can be put with other pieces, and stained glass can be created into something beautiful. Remember that we are allowed to fall apart sometimes. But it's finding our pieces and making something beautiful out of it.

_____

_____

_____

_____

_____

_____

_____

_____

_____

_____

_____

_____

_____

_____

_____

_____

Spontaneous

Two wet feet,
Jump up and hang on.

There will be ups,
There will be downs.
But this will be an incredible journey.

Spontaneous.

Is this right?
Or is this going to not be good?

Life is a journey.
Make choices. Make decisions.

Be spontaneous.

Two wet feet,
Jump in and hang on.

This will be the best for you!

There comes at least one time in your life that you wish you had been spontaneous or wanted to be. Here's a place to write a time that you've wanted to be and something spontaneous that you have always wanted to do.

_____

_____

_____

_____

_____

_____

_____

_____

_____

_____

_____

_____

_____

_____

_____

_____

_____

_____

Untitled

Every line,

Every word.

The thoughts,

The emotions.

Every line is put together with heart.

Speak to your soul.

Read the words,

Each and every line.

Make you feel,

Make you smile,

Make you cry.

The love and emotions,

Flow like blood in your veins.

Make you think,

Make you reflect.

Take the time,

Read each line,

All the words are there,

Let them into your soul.

Feel the emotions,

Enjoy the lines.

Untitled…… well, what to say about this…. I tried for many, many hours to find a title for this one and couldn't. The saying goes. Sometimes, you can't find the words. Here, you can let them out.

_____

_____

_____

_____

_____

_____

_____

_____

_____

_____

_____

_____

_____

_____

_____

_____

_____

_____

Falling

The ground seems so far away.

I can feel the wind against my arms.

All these emotions,

All the tension,

All the stress.

Everything that is happening right now.

I'm falling,

Falling so fast,

I am afraid of what is going to happen.

Once I hit the bottom,

Will I be able to get up?

Will anyone be there to catch me?

Or will I be alone?

I am falling into a place I never thought I would end up back into.

I am falling so fast.

I'm afraid of what I might do.

I am falling so

FAST

And it's all because of you.

Here, I fell back in love. Something I didn't think would ever happen. Sometimes, life will happen at the most unexpected times. Live the unexpected. Love the unexpected. Sometimes, the most wonderful things are the outcomes when we don't expect anything. You are always allowed to fall in and out of love with yourself or anyone, for that matter. Love is such a beautiful thing. It's always there. Sometimes just hidden.

Through the window

Looking through the window,
I see those big brown eyes,
Searching out into the distance.
Do you see what you are looking for?

A smile,

Your eyes light up.
The clouds go away, and the sun comes out.
The pure joy and love,
is expressed on your face.

As the sun's rays get warmer and warmer,
You look through the window.

That flower that you have been watching from afar,
is blooming.

The sun shines.
And petal by petal,
It blooms.

Through the window as you watch.

Words

Every single one.
Do you think before they come out of your mouth?

Do you think before they are expressed in letters?

Words.

They can have the most positive impact,
Or trap negativity in your mind.

Those words
Keep them to yourself.
Can you not see what they are doing?
Does this look fun to you?

Every single one.
Whether they are written or spoken,
Please keep them away.

Those little minds and hearts,
Are hurting.

All because of
Those words.

Words. All the words you feel and want to write. Here's your place!

_____

_____

_____

_____

_____

_____

_____

_____

_____

_____

_____

_____

_____

_____

_____

_____

_____

_____

I'll be there

Every time,
When you think no one will be.

I'll be there.

When you are at your highest,
When you are at your lowest.
When you are angry,
Or want to fall apart.
When you feel like you've won the lottery,
Or have the most exciting news.

I'll be there.
Is that okay?

I'll be there in the morning,
I'll be there in the night.
Whenever you need me,
I'll be there.

I'll remind you with words,
I'll remind you with actions.

Please remember,
I'll always be there.

The words I'll be there...that's what friends are for. We all live in our own worlds sometimes and meeting new people can be scary. Try and get yourself out there and meet a new friend. Say hello to people more often. It just lets people know that there's good in the world. Even just the phrase I hope you have a good day.

Here's a challenge: tell people who you don't know each month to have a good day. Keep count on how many people you try and encourage.

_____

_____

_____

_____

_____

_____

_____

_____

_____

_____

_____

_____

_____

_____

_____

_____

It's okay

If you don't want to talk,

If you just want to lay here.

Just lay in my arms for a while.

It's okay.

If you want to tell me what is going on,

If you feel like you just want to let go.

If you want to cry,

Or scream,

Or just talk.

It's okay.

When you are ready, I will tell you it's okay.

You are allowed to feel,

You are allowed to have emotions,

It's okay.

You'll be okay.

Don't give up

The track you are on,
You're falling behind.

Don't give up.

Take one task at a time,
One challenge complete,
Move to the next.

When you feel like you are going nowhere,
Stuck in the same place.

Don't give up.

You're trying to move too fast,
You must slow down.
The steps you are climbing are too far away.
Smaller steps will get you to the same place.

Please
Don't give up.

You are already a success,
Even when you don't feel it.

All because,

You didn't give up!

The last two poems acknowledge that it is okay to not be okay, but you can't give up on yourself. What are some strategies that you have in place for yourself when you are not okay?

_____

_____

_____

_____

_____

_____

_____

_____

_____

_____

_____

_____

_____

_____

_____

_____

_____

_____

Gone

It was too late.

You should have tried.

I gave up,

And now I am gone.

Gone,

Not coming back.

You can't catch me,

I've gone too far.

Please don't try,

It's too late.

Too many promises broken,

Too many lies told.

Too many I'm sorries,

Not enough love.

Gone.

Gone are the days I won't be loved.

Gone are the days I'll be lied to.

Gone are the forgiven I'm sorries.

Gone in the past.

Gone.

It's too late.

I'm gone and not coming back.

Goodbye.

Life doesn't always bloom like roses. People come and people go. Sometimes, you go in the same direction and sometimes in opposite directions. Sometimes, you must walk away from people in your life in order to do what's best for yourself in order to grow. Is there a time when you had to do that? Is there anyone in your life now that you are drifting apart from? Is there someone new in your life who is showing there is more in life to offer you?

_____

_____

_____

_____

_____

_____

_____

_____

_____

_____

_____

_____

_____

_____

_____

_____

Learn

Take it in,
Every moment,
Every lesson.
Learn.

Learn from every chance, choice, and decision you make.
Learn from others,
Learn from yourself.

Be encouraged to learn,
And encourage others in return.

You are worth the knowledge,
And acknowledging this worth.

You are learning!

Learn the knowledge you receive.
It can be provided to others so they can learn.

Learn from your mistakes,
Learn from your growth,
Learn for your dreams.

If there is but one thing I hope that is don't with this book, I hope you learn. Learn about yourself. Learn to love and learn to live. Here is a section to reflect and put down what you have learned.

_____

_____

_____

_____

_____

_____

_____

_____

_____

_____

_____

_____

_____

_____

_____

_____

_____

_____

The wait

There you are,

Standing there in that gown,

Here, I am standing 5 feet away.

Waiting.

The emotions and words from your heart,

Tears of love stream down your cheeks.

As I hold your hand in mine,

The thought crossed my mind.

What if I didn't wait?

We would not be standing here today.

We waited,

We fought,

We conquered.

And here we are standing here today.

I'll always wait.

Everyday,

Every night,

Every smile,

Every tear.

This love,

This moment,

The pure joy in my heart.

Was worth the wait.

My fight

Every day, I learn,

I hang on,

I take deep breaths,

I fight to get through the day.

Myself,

You,

Them,

Everyday.

My mind fights with me.

My emotions fight with me.

My heart fights with me.

I feel my fight with life gets harder some days.

But my fight could be worse.

I still have life left to fight for.

I have myself,

I have you,

I have them.

Everyday.

I will fight my fight,

I am strong.

This is mine,

I will conquer it.

We all have our own battles with life. Some of us struggle more than others. Some of us have more support, while some have better coping skills. I hope this book has given you some tools and insight to learn other outlooks on life. Here's a spot for you to write out for yourself to see what you have learned.

_____

_____

_____

_____

_____

_____

_____

_____

_____

_____

_____

_____

_____

_____

_____

_____

_____

The start

As you sit there shaking,

I'll hold out my hand.

Pull you near,

Move your hair from your face.

You whisper, "This is the end."

As I lift up your chin,

And look into your eyes and say,

"No, this is the start."

You will no longer be hurt,

You will no longer be afraid.

This is the start.

The start of your new life,

The start of the new you.

The start of a whole new world.

There is no end in sight for you,

The light begins to relight the life in your eyes.

Step by step,

Day by day.

Darling,

This is just the start.

Every day we wake up, we are given a new opportunity to change ourselves. It's up to us how we choose to live our lives, what we choose to do with ourselves, and who we include. What are some things that you might want differently or what you like to stay?

_____

_____

_____

_____

_____

_____

_____

_____

_____

_____

_____

_____

_____

_____

_____

_____

_____

_____

Pain is real, embrace it

First, I lost him,

Then I lost you,

Then I lost her.

Almost lost myself along the way.

Every day, I want you back,

Reality sets in, knowing it's never possible.

Now,

I have them,

I have me.

Yes,

Pain is real, embrace it.

Open your arms wide open,

And know in your body, mind, and soul.

That you can and will get through it.

Someone somewhere will be there.

Someone somewhere is going through a dark, tough time.

Someone somewhere won't make it through.

Be that someone you once had,

When you needed them.

Embrace them. Their pain is real.

Knowing that I haven't truly lost everything,

You are still in my body, mind, soul, and heart.

I continue to embrace the pain.

Remain real in life,

Share my embrace with those who are in pain.

Sometimes, when we are hurting, a hug can go a long way. When we are embraced, hormones are released, and we become more content. This section is going to be both a self-reflection and a challenge. Does a hug make you feel better? And have you hugged someone in hopes of making them feel better? The next time someone is not doing well, wrap your arms around them and give them a hug. And if they ask why, just tell them sometimes we just need a hug.

_____

_____

_____

_____

_____

_____

_____

_____

_____

_____

_____

_____

_____

_____

_____

_____

_____

_____

This feeling

One step at a time,
Overcome every challenge,
Every obstacle to get here.

Each piece so much thought,
So much love,
Release of emotions,
Encourage positivity.
Develop growth.
Motivate.

But this feeling.

It's more than that.
When I felt like a mouse in a room,
Now, the light shines on me!

This feeling is incredible,
This feeling will be unstoppable.

This is the best feeling.
Amazing, incredible, desirable.

Here,
I want to give you all this feeling, too.
You got this,

This feeling.

Writing out anything can leave you with the feeling of being vulnerable. It can be scary, it can be exciting, but most of all, it can be very rewarding. Opening my poetry to the world in hopes of one day making a difference in just one person's life. My hope is that person is you, the one who is taking the time out of your day to read this book. I just want to thank you. I believe in you. No matter what you might be going through in your life, what you have gone through does not determine who you will become. You do! You are most capable of anything you set your mind to.

Writing this book has taught me that I can live life and overcome obstacles and that I will show my children to believe in a dream that they have and that they can accomplish it. It is okay to put things to the side when your life becomes too busy, but if it's a dream that you are truly passionate about when the time is right, life has its plan to put that dream back into your path and make you get back to working on it. I often tell people sometimes, when you are walking down the path called life, it is okay to take a few steps back to have more options for pathways to choose further down the path. If you are on a narrow path, you won't see any options. If you step back, some new ones might become available. When the path is dark, look for the light. It will be there. You might have to take it slow. You might need help along the way; don't be afraid to ask.

In closing, once again, thank you to all who have crossed my path, helped me to pursue my dream, and believed in me. I hope that all my readers achieve at least one dream in their lives! And remember, don't ever lose hope!

Cheyanne Cramm

Manufactured by Amazon.ca
Acheson, AB